D0350307

DU

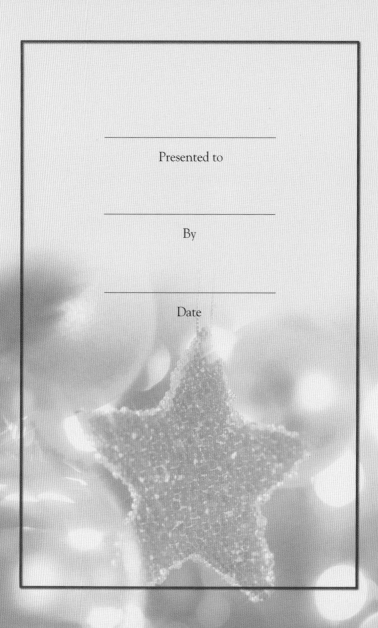

_____

Presented to

_____

By

_____

Date

the most Wonderful time of the year

There is born to you this day in the city of
David a Savior, who is Christ the Lord.

LUKE 2:11 NKJV

the most *Wonderful* time of *the* year

101 INSPIRING WAYS TO ENJOY *Christmas*

CANDY PAULL

HOWARD BOOKS

A DIVISION OF SIMON & SCHUSTER

New York   London   Toronto   Sydney

Our purpose at Howard Books is to:

Increase faith in the hearts of growing Christians

Inspire holiness in the lives of believers

Instill hope in the hearts of struggling people everywhere

Because He's coming again!

Published by Howard Books, a division of Simon & Schuster, Inc.
1230 Avenue of the Americas, New York, NY 10020
www.howardpublishing.com

The Most Wonderful Time of the Year © 2009 by GRQ, Inc.

ISBN 978-1-4165-9858-9

10 9 8 7 6 5 4 3 2 1

HOWARD and colophon are registered trademarks of Simon & Schuster, Inc.

Manufactured in China

For information regarding special discounts for bulk purchases, please contact: Simon & Schuster Special Sales at 1-866-506-1949 or business@simonandschuster.com.

The Simon & Schuster Speakers Bureau can bring authors to your live event. For more information or to book an event, contact the Simon & Schuster Speakers Bureau at 1-866-248-3049 or visit our website at www.simonspeakers.com.

Managing Editor: Lila Empson
Associate Editor: Chrys Howard
Design: Whisner Design Group
Photo credits: Shutterstock, iPhoto, and Getty Images

Scripture quotations noted CEV are from the Contemporary English Version Copyright © 1995 by American Bible Society. Used by permission. Scripture quotations noted MSG are from *The Message*. Copyright © by Eugene H. Peterson 1993, 1994, 1995, 1996, 2000, 2001, 2002. Used by permission of NavPress Publishing Group. Scripture quotations noted NIV are from the Holy Bible: New International Version®. Copyright © 1973, 1978, 1984 by International Bible Society. Used by permission of Zondervan Publishing House. All rights reserved. Scripture quotations noted NKJV are from The New King James Version®. Copyright © 1979, 1980, 1982 by Thomas Nelson, Inc. Used by permission. All rights reserved. Scripture quotations noted NLT are from the *Holy Bible*, New Living Translation, copyright © 1996, 2004. Used by permission of Tyndale House Publishers, Inc., Wheaton, Illinois 60189. All rights reserved.

Contents

Contents

Contents

Contents

Christmas

Christmas is not just a day, an event to be observed and speedily forgotten. It is a spirit which should permeate every part of our lives. To believe that the spirit of Christmas does change lives and to labor for the realization of its coming to all men is the essence of our faith in Christ.

WILLIAM PARKS

$\mathscr{I}$NTRODUCTION

Christmas can be a wonderful time of year. Getting together with loved ones, giving gifts, and celebrating favorite traditions are just a few of the things to love about this special season.

Christmas from the Heart offers simple ideas for making the season brighter and merrier. From singing favorite carols to sharing lots of hugs, from finding the perfect gift to baking Christmas treats, you will be reminded that there are many wonderful activities and experiences you can create and savor.

It is also a reminder to keep the spirit of Christmas in your heart by living in the presence of God, slowing down, taking time to give to those in need, and remembering what the birth of Christ really means. May the love of God be the benediction in everything you do and say during this wondrous and joyous time of year.

It is Christmas in the heart that puts Christmas in the air.

W. T. ELLIS

The Word became flesh and blood, and moved into the neighborhood. We saw the glory with our own eyes, the one-of-a-kind glory, like Father, like Son, generous inside and out, true from start to finish.
John 1:14 MSG

A Christmas Prayer

As we celebrate the birth of Christ, let our hearts be tender and our hands work for the peace of all. May we honor him by loving one another as God so loved the world when he gave his beloved Son.

May we receive all the gifts that the season has to offer with open hands and grateful hearts. And may we cherish the beauty of this season, treasuring the moments and creating memories that will bless us for the rest of our lives.

AMEN

1

Remember the Reason for the Season

Christmas is a time of color, excitement, beauty, and tradition. In the midst of shopping for the perfect gift, decorating the tree, and gathering with loved ones, take time to remember the reason for the season. This year, make your Christmas more meaningful by meditating on the life of the Christ child who was born in that stable in Bethlehem two thousand years ago.

Read a Christmas devotional book that takes you through the season and talks about what God's love means in your life today. Meditate on the meaning of God in human form, bringing transforming love to every aspect of your life here and now.

The Word of God, Jesus Christ, on account of his great love for mankind, became what we are in order to make us what he is himself.

SAINT IRENAEUS

Remember

Sing (or read) all the verses of famous carols like "It Came upon the Midnight Clear" or "Silent Night" to remind yourself of the true meaning of Christmas.

1

2

*M*ake a *C*hild *H*appy

Joy

❧

Set aside some extra money to spend on a special child or children in your life. Give the gift of your time and attention as well as material gifts.

❧

It's wonderful to watch a child's face light up with joy. With just a little time and attention, you can give a gift that sets a child's eyes twinkling. You can "adopt" a child, or a whole family, for the season. Take children out for a special treat and listen to their hopes and dreams—then give a gift that makes at least one wish come true.

It doesn't take much to make a child happy. A listening heart and the treasure of your time and attention are the most meaningful gifts. You'll receive great joy when you make Christmas merrier for the little ones.

*I will sing of the mercies of the L*ORD *forever;*
with my mouth will I make known Your
faithfulness to all generations.

PSALM 89:1 NKJV

Christmas Spirit

Until one feels the spirit of Christmas, there is no Christmas. All else is outward display—so much tinsel and decorations. For it isn't the holly, it isn't the snow. It isn't the tree, not the firelight's glow. It's the warmth that comes to the hearts of men when the Christmas spirit returns again.

AUTHOR UNKNOWN

3
Make a Wish List

Wish

Include a favorite charity on your wish list so you can make someone else's wishes come true.

Ask any child what he or she wants for Christmas, and you'll usually get a long list of heart's desires. Wish lists come naturally to the human heart, whether it's for a new toy or for peace on earth.

This Christmas, make a different kind of wish list. Instead of listing things that you want, ask loved ones to make a wish list of what they would like to receive and what prayers they would like answered. Make your wish list a prayer list, too. Whether it's a material need or a cry of the heart, pray for wisdom and guidance. Then give thanks for the answer that will come.

Keep on asking, and you will receive what you ask for. Keep on seeking, and you will find. Keep on knocking, and the door will be opened to you.

MATTHEW 7:7 NLT

4
Enjoy Poetry, Stories, and Songs

Whether it's another chorus of "Jingle Bell Rock" or a choir singing "It Came upon the Midnight Clear," the music of Christmas is the signal that the season is upon us. Stories of Christmas morning with Louisa May Alcott's *Little Women* and the sacrificial giving of O. Henry's young couple in *The Gift of the Magi* are reminders that Christmas is about love and giving.

Invest in a collection of seasonal stories, a new Christmas music CD, or a book of poems and meditations that bring fresh insight to the meaning of this time of year. Relish the once-a-year fun of old favorites and new creative delights.

I truly believe that if we keep telling the Christ-mas story, singing the Christmas songs, and living the Christmas spirit, we can bring joy and happiness and peace to this world.

NORMAN VINCENT PEALE

Host a Christmas reading party where each person brings a favorite story, poem, or song to share.

5

Celebrate Advent

Promise

Buy or make an
Advent calendar. Set
up a Nativity scene on
a table or a special
place of honor in
your home.

A modern commercial Christmas begins with store decorations and ends with gifts under the tree. But Advent has been celebrated for centuries by the church, and its ceremonies and traditions provide a way to meditate on the true meaning of Christmas. A time for Christians to think about God's promises, Advent prepares the heart for the celebration of Christ's birth on Christmas Day.

From the fourth Sunday before Christmas through Christmas Eve, take time each day to celebrate Advent. There are Advent devotionals and calendars available to take you through the season. Let this time be a quiet anticipation to prepare your heart for Christmas.

The birth of Jesus is the sunrise of the Bible.

HENRY VAN DYKE

Touch Hands

Ah friends, dear friends,
as years go on and heads get gray,
how fast the guests do go!
Touch hands, touch hands,
with those who stay.
Strong hands to weak,
old hands to young,
around the Christmas board
touch hands.

WILLIAM H. MURRAY

6

Read the Christmas Story Aloud

Hear

Enjoy an imaginative rendering of the Christmas story by Walter Wangerin Jr. in his classic retelling of biblical stories, *The Book of God.*

"And it came to pass in those days that a decree went out from Caesar Augustus that all the world should be registered" begins the book of Luke, chapter 2, verse 1 (NKJV). Whether you read the Christmas story in the majestic syllables of the King James version of Luke 2:1–16 or in a modern Bible version with contemporary language, the Christmas story is timeless.

Set aside some time with family, friends, or loved ones to share the Christmas story. Read aloud and let the story of Mary, Joseph, and the baby Jesus touch your heart through the spoken word.

She gave birth to her first-born son. She dressed him in baby clothes and laid him on a bed of hay, because there was no room for them in the inn.

LUKE 2:7 CEV

7

Lend a Helping Hand

The only hands God has are your hands. It is through your actions that he reaches out to those who need a helping hand and a caring touch. This Christmas, make it a point to lend a helping hand to others. Make it a priority to include, along with the gift giving and celebrations, the part of Christmas that reflects God's love for the world in practical ways.

Decorate the church or feed the homeless at a soup kitchen. Offer to help your hostess clean up. Look for small services you can give that will make others' lives just a little bit easier.

It is possible to give without loving, but it is impossible to love without giving.

RICHARD BRAUNSTEIN

Help

Be alert for opportunities to lend a hand, from opening doors and carrying groceries to volunteering at a local charity.

Joyous Life

If we are ever to enjoy life, now is the time—not tomorrow, nor next year, nor in some future life after we have died. The best preparation for a better life next year is a full, complete, harmonious, joyous life this year. Our beliefs in a rich future life are of little importance unless we coin them into a rich present life. Today should always be our most wonderful day.

THOMAS DREIER

8

Delight in the *Details*

Lights reflected in a Christmas ball on the tree. Scented paperwhite narcissi bringing a touch of spring amid the evergreens. The sound of carolers and the crackle of wrapping paper as you tie a ribbon around a gift for someone you love. If God is in the details, this is especially true around Christmastime.

Savor the small things, for they speak to your heart most deeply. Like the Christ child who nestled in his mother's arms in an obscure part of the Roman Empire, the most meaningful moments of Christmas come not in pomp and circumstance, but in the small gifts each moment offers.

Ordinary things have great power to reveal the mysterious nearness of a caring, liberating God.

CHARLES CUMMINGS

Delight

Be alert for your favorite things during this season. Take notice of sights, scents, sounds, and textures that offer delight.

9
Host a Dessert Party

Festive

Ask guests to bring a favorite inspirational quote or Scripture verse and have them share what it means to them personally.

Not up for a big dinner or a complicated party? Why not host a simple dessert get-together with friends and family? Instead of feeling overwhelmed by elaborate preparations, you can enjoy spending time with loved ones and nibbling festive goodies made by other hands.

Set a pretty table; offer coffee, tea, and punch; and ask everybody to bring their favorite dessert or special Christmas cookies. Play seasonal music in the background. You may want to have different people bring a reading to share for entertainment. By keeping it simple, you'll make it easy for everyone to enjoy Christmas a little bit more this year.

Christmas is the season for kindling the fire of hospitality in the hall, the genial flame of charity in the heart.

Washington Irving

Gracious Season

Some say that ever 'gainst that season comes

Wherein our Saviour's birth is celebrated,

The bird of dawning singeth all night long:

And then, they say, no spirit dare stir abroad;

The nights are wholesome, then no planets strike . . .

So hallow'd and so gracious is the time.

WILLIAM SHAKESPEARE

10

Stay in Touch with Loved Ones

Make it a point to call someone you haven't talked with in a long time. Take delight in hearing your friend's voice on the phone and catching up.

It's so easy to lose touch with one another in today's busy world. Christmas is a wonderful season to make staying in touch a priority and to reconnect with those you love. It's a natural time to call or write, letting people know that you think they are very special and important in your life.

A Christmas card, a phone call, a small gift, or an invitation to share a meal can all help you stay in touch. No matter how far away they may be, there are many ways to stay connected to those you love. Let Christmas remind you to do so.

Sometimes our light goes out but is blown into flame by another human being. Each of us owes deepest thanks to those who have rekindled this light.

ALBERT SCHWEITZER

11

Take Time for Quiet Contemplation

There is a quiet place, far from the rapid pace, where God can touch your heart and soothe your spirit. When the hectic rush of the season swirls around you, take time away for some quiet prayer and contemplation. It will become a vital lifeline between you and God, anchoring your spirit in the midst of a busy season.

Make it a point to spend a few minutes each day alone to breathe deeply, still your soul, and allow God to speak to your heart. You'll return from your time of contemplation refreshed and rested, ready to enjoy Christmas activities with a renewed zest.

> *I have given rest to the weary*
> *and joy to the sorrowing.*
>
> JEREMIAH 31:25 NLT

Retreat to a quiet nook to read, pray, and meditate. Light a candle as a reminder that this is a sacred time between you and God.

Love that Lives

Every child on earth is holy,

Every crib is a manger lowly,

Every home is a stable dim,

Every kind word is a hymn,

Every star is God's own gem,

And every town is Bethlehem

For Christ is born again and again,

When His love lives in the hearts of men.

W. D. DORRITY

12

Simplify Your Celebration

When you feel that Christmas is going to overwhelm you with too many parties, too much to do, and too few moments to relax, consider the possibility that a simpler Christmas celebration may be more meaningful. Remind yourself that Christmas is not about performance, but about simple joys and the ability to share love.

Pare down your obligations and simplify your celebration. Instead of trying to do and be everything, say no to elaborate preparations and choose easier, simpler ways to savor the season. Do less, buy less, and create space for more heartfelt moments of celebration that speak to the heart.

Probably the reason we all go haywire at Christmas time with the endless unrestrained and often silly buying of gifts is that we don't quite know how to put our love into words.

HARLAN MILLER

Simplify

Simplify Christmas by committing to one less event this year. Use the time saved for rest, reflection, or simply enjoying more time with loved ones.

13

Write a Personal Christmas Prayer

Pray

Use calligraphy or an elegant type to create a copy of your prayer on high-quality paper. Decorate it and frame it as a reminder to pray.

Prayer is at the heart of Christmas. It is a time when God's coming to earth to be with humanity is celebrated and remembered. So take some time to talk with the God who loves you so much that he gave his only Son.

One way to make your Christmas prayer time more meaningful is by writing a personal prayer to use during the season. In your prayer, recognize that God loves you and that you are in communion with him. Rejoice in the gift of his love, release your worries to him, and praise him for all that he is doing in your life.

Pray in the Spirit on all occasions with all kinds of prayers and requests.

EPHESIANS 6:18 NIV

14

Send a Christmas Newsletter

Christmas newsletters are becoming more popular all the time. They are quick ways to catch distant friends and relatives up on all the family doings. A newsy recap of who's been doing what can let people know about important events that have happened in your life in the last year.

You can make your Christmas newsletter special by being a bit more open and vulnerable. Along with your list of accomplishments, include a personal life lesson learned or a difficult time weathered. You don't have to go into gritty detail, but the human touch is always welcome. Include a photo for others to enjoy.

The angel said to them, "Do not be afraid, for behold, I bring you good tidings of great joy which will be to all people."

LUKE 2:10 NKJV

Write

Create an e-newsletter that includes photos and links that help tell the story of your Christmas adventures.

Love in Action

Christmas, my child, is love in action. Every time we love, every time we give, it's Christmas.

DALE EVANS ROGERS

May the Lord make your love for one another and for all people grow and overflow, just as our love for you overflows.

1 THESSALONIANS 3:12 NLT

15

Go Christmas Caroling

Voices blending in harmony make a beautiful sound. Even if you're not the lead soprano in the choir or the tenor soloist who moves audiences to tears, you can still enjoy sharing the gift of song together with others. Familiar Christmas carols are fun to sing and make it easy for everyone to join in on the chorus.

Singing Christmas songs brings people together in the spirit of the season. It feels wonderful to blend voices together harmoniously, and the words of the traditional carols often hold deep spiritual lessons. Sing all the verses of your favorite carols and discover the rich meaning in the songs.

Go caroling with friends around the neighborhood. Bring some chocolate kisses to pass around or confetti to toss to add to the celebratory spirit.

Forth they went and glad they were,
Going they did sing;
With mirth and solace they made good cheer
For joy of that new tiding.

COVENTRY NATIVITY PLAY (A.D. 1200)

16

Give a Gift Anonymously

One source of Christmas delight is the anonymous gift. This kind of giving puts a little mystery into the act of spreading good cheer. Whether it's a simple note of encouragement, a food basket left on a needy family's doorstep, or the anonymous gift of cash in an envelope, finding ways to get a gift to someone without letting them know who gave it can be a lot of fun.

Choose someone you know who needs special encouragement and create a gift that speaks to his or her need—then deliver it anonymously.

When you give anonymously, only God knows who the giver is. There is no obligation, no need for fanfare. The person receiving the gift only knows that somehow, somewhere, someone was thinking of them.

Be careful not to do your "acts of righteousness" before men, to be seen by them. If you do, you will have no reward from your Father in heaven.

MATTHEW 6:1 NIV

A Time to Share

At this season, let us be mindful of each other. Let us know the shelter of one another. Let us be the angels we have heard so much about.

CORRINE DE WINTER

Make each day useful and cheerful and prove that you know the worth of time by employing it well. Then youth will be happy, old age without regret, and life a beautiful success.

LOUISA MAY ALCOTT

17

*M*ake a *S*hopping *L*ist

Plan

❧

Make one shopping list for gifts and one for home and party necessities to help you sort priorities and keep things straight.

❧

Make your Christmas buying easier by making a shopping list. Because there are so many tempting distractions in stores at Christmastime, a shopping list can help keep you on track and on budget. It's like a compass that can guide you safely through the aisles of the stores to find that perfect gift for that perfect someone in your life.

Your shopping list reflects your values, as well. Seek quality instead of quantity. Thoughtful gifts reflect an inner generosity. Planning and careful spending habits help you use your resources wisely. Let the choices you make with material things reflect the spiritual values you live by.

You will understand what is right and just and fair—every good path.

PROVERBS 2:9 NIV

18
Bake Cookies Together

Christmas is the perfect time to teach a young apprentice the fine art of baking cookies together. Little hands can sift flour, shape dough, and decorate the cookies. Precious Christmas memories are made when you share the fun with little ones. A simple cooking lesson may have an impact on a child's life that lives on years after the last cookie has been eaten.

Even grown-ups are like children when it comes to baking (and eating!) cookies, so invite friends to help with cookie creation. Turn it into a baking party. Make double batches of cookies so that everyone can take some home.

A house is not a home unless it contains food and fire for the mind as well as the body.

MARGARET FULLER

Bake

Try at least one new cookie recipe along with the old favorites. It could become another classic family favorite.

The Welcoming Heart

Every humble human heart may be
the birthplace of a Christ Child if it is
not too crowded like the inn at Bethlehem. If the heart is open, no matter
if toil and care are stabled there and
the cradle is only lined with the straw
of the fields, the ideal of brotherhood,
nurtured by unselfishness and love,
will be born and the Star of Promise
will light the path of a new hope.

HERBERT L. SATTERLEE

19

Celebrate Your Friendships

She's been your best friend for years, sharing all your important secrets. He's stood by you through tough times. And you have fabulous new friends who have brought fresh interests and viewpoints into your life. So what better time to enjoy the friends who are God's gift to you than in this season of good cheer?

Celebrate your friendships during the Christmas season. It's a special time of year and a special reason to get together. Meet a friend for lunch, host a get-together to introduce friends to one another, and create cards, gifts, and remembrances that say to dear friends, "You're important to me."

Just as lotions and fragrance give sensual delight, a sweet friendship refreshes the soul.

PROVERBS 27:9 MSG

Meet

Set up a time to get together with a friend for coffee and an exchange of gifts. Make it a delightful break away from busy schedules.

20

Decorate with Light

Glow

Put up Christmas lights in early December to make your home beautiful. Decorate a mantel or table with glowing candles.

At the darkest time of the year, Christmas is the season that celebrates light and life. As the solstice marks the longest night of the year, Advent and Christmas remind us that God's love is as sure as the sunrise. Colorful lights, glowing candles, and starry skies are reminders that the darkness can never put out the light.

Decorate your home with light. Put twinkling lights on the Christmas tree, light tapers that will shine like living stars in the house, and let dark windows reflect the warm glow of firelight in a cozy living room. Be lavish and light up the night with light.

You were once darkness, but now you are light in the Lord. Live as children of light.

EPHESIANS 5:8 NIV

Circle of Love

Time was with most of us, when Christmas Day, encircling all our limited world like a magic ring, left nothing out for us to miss or seek; bound together all our home enjoyments, affections, and hopes; grouped everything and everyone round the Christmas fire, and made the little picture shining in our bright young eyes, complete.

CHARLES DICKENS

21

Create a Christmas Memory Book

Memories

Explore a craft store for scrapbook ideas and supplies and create a one-of-a-kind personal memory book this year.

You always think you'll remember the special moments that each Christmas brings. But memories have to be kept as well as made, or they will be lost in the mists of time. Put some of those remembrances between the pages of a memory book. Then you can return to Christmas past and relive treasured memories again.

Buy or make a special cover for this book. Include photos, mementos, and journal entries. Personal reminiscences, handwritten notes, even shopping lists and greeting cards can be included. Create a collage of Christmas memories that you will never forget.

Christmas may be a day of feasting, or of prayer, but always it will be a day of remembrance—a day in which we think of everything we have ever loved.

AUGUSTA E. RUNDEL

22

Look Up at the Stars

The stars are wheeling overhead, pinpoints of light in an infinite darkness. There is something splendid and awesome about staring up at a starry sky and feeling how small you are in the light of eternity. Though you feel smaller under that canopy of open sky, you also know that the God who created all those stars is here with you, in human heart and human home.

Go outside. Take advantage of a clear winter night sky to look up at the stars and down into your heart. Be reminded that life is greater than it sometimes appears. Remember who you are under the stars.

It takes solitude, under the stars, for us to be reminded of our eternal origin and our far destiny.

ARCHIBALD RUTLEDGE

Vision

Put your coat on and go stargaze for at least a few minutes on a clear, cold night. Also enjoy the view of lighted windows before you go back inside.

23
Take a Nap

Sleep

❦

Invest in an herbal eye
pillow. It will help you
relax and close out
the world for a
few minutes.

If you are feeling tired and frazzled, take a few minutes to refresh yourself with a quick nap. It can be a brief catnap in a chair or a real lie-down with comforter and pillow on your bed. As you rest your body, you renew your spirit. And then you can go on to the next activity in your day with energy and good cheer.

If you're especially tired, set aside time for a longer, deeper nap. Getting extra zzz's will help you cope with Christmas schedules and stress. Remember that naps are not just for children—grown-ups need them, too.

I will lie down and sleep in peace, for you alone, O LORD, make me dwell in safety.

PSALM 4:8 NIV

One Child

More light than we can learn,

More wealth than we can treasure,

More love than we can earn,

More peace than we can measure,

Because one Child is born.

AUTHOR UNKNOWN

24

Dress Up

Sparkle

Tie a red ribbon around a sprig of holly or evergreen and pin it on your lapel for an inexpensive and festive seasonal touch.

With its many parties and get-togethers, Christmas offers plenty of reasons to dress up. But you don't need an elaborate party outfit—just adding simple seasonal touches to your everyday clothing can dress you up for the holidays.

Celebrate Christmas in red and green, or with rich burgundy and gold. When you bring the colors of the season into your wardrobe, you bring a celebratory touch to everything you wear. It can be as simple as a bright woolen scarf or a sparkly brooch, or as elaborate as an elegant velvet ensemble that lifts your spirits every time you put it on.

God's fingers can touch nothing but to mold it into loveliness.

GEORGE MACDONALD

25

Pray for Peace on Earth

The angels sang to the shepherds at Christ's birth, "Peace on earth, goodwill to humanity." Christmastide is a reminder that peace on earth is God's desire for all of his children. In a world of fear and violence, it is a radical act to pray for peace. Yet your prayers for peace have never been more necessary.

Prayer works. You may not see a cause-and-effect answer to your prayers every time, but it is always worthwhile to pray. As the Christ child came to bring peace to troubled human hearts, you can help it happen by praying earnestly for peace on earth.

You're blessed when you can show people how to cooperate instead of compete or fight. That's when you discover who you really are, and your place in God's family.

MATTHEW 5:9 MSG

Peace

Meet with others to pray for peace as often as you can. There are many churches and organizations that hold peace vigils and services.

Christmas Wonder

Infinite, and an infant. Eternal, and yet born of a woman. Almighty, and yet hanging on a woman's breast. Supporting a universe, and yet needing to be carried in a mother's arms. King of angels, and yet the reputed son of Joseph. Heir of all things, and yet the carpenter's despised son. Oh, the wonder of Christmas.

CHARLES HADDON SPURGEON

26

*C*elebrate a *N*atural *C*hristmas

As an antidote to the frenzied glitter of commercial Christmas, seek out ways to create a natural celebration. Forgo the plastic wreaths, bizarrely blinking aluminum trees, and the artificial excess and gaudiness. Instead, rediscover the gentle magic of natural-looking arrangements made from found objects and greens gathered from the wild.

From using recycled papers to decorating a live tree that can be planted after Christmas, you can demonstrate practical concern for the earth. You'll feel more in tune with the rhythms of creation as the gentle grace and beauty of nature remind you of God's timing and goodness in your life.

Nature is the art of God Eternal.

Dante Alighieri

Grow

Make a natural wreath of evergreens and pinecones or grapevines and berries for your front door or entryway.

37

27

Give Homemade Gifts

Make

If you have a special craft that you enjoy, create Christmas presents during the year that you've made with your own two loving hands.

🍂

Homemade gifts were usually the only gifts available on the prairie back in the days of Laura Ingalls Wilder's childhood. Simple, but created with love and care, those gifts were treasured because of who had made them. Homemade gifts were rich with love, even if they didn't cost a lot of money to make.

If you love arts, crafts, or cooking, enjoy the pleasure of using your skills to create one-of-a-kind gifts for friends and family. A hand-knit scarf, a loaf of pumpkin bread, blackberry jam put up last summer, a keepsake box made of exquisite heartwood—all of these handmade, homemade gifts make Christmas even sweeter.

> *I am beginning to learn that it is the sweet, simple things of life which are the real ones after all.*

> LAURA INGALLS WILDER

A Child's Spirit

Our religion is one which challenges the ordinary human standards by holding that the ideal of life is the spirit of a little child. We tend to glorify adulthood and wisdom and worldly prudence, but the Gospel reverses all this. The Gospel says that the inescapable condition of entrance into the divine fellowship is that we turn and become as a little child.

ELTON TRUEBLOOD

28

Enjoy Christmas Classics

Pleasure

Host a dramatic reading of A *Christmas Carol* or other Christmas story or play, with each person taking a part. You could even dress in character.

"God bless us every one," says Tiny Tim in the Charles Dickens story *A Christmas Carol*. Ebenezer Scrooge, Clement Clarke Moore's "The Night Before Christmas," or O. Henry's "The Gift of the Magi" all kindle images of Christmas in the heart. Going to see a performance of *The Nutcracker* or Handel's *Messiah* are important Christmas traditions in many people's lives.

It's fun to try new things, but certain pleasures grow with repetition. Enjoy the once-a-year performances and make room in your busy schedule for at least one of the familiar Christmas classics that never grow old, but grow sweeter every year.

Then Bob proposed: "A Merry Christmas to us all, my dears. God bless us!" Which all his family re-echoed. "God bless us every one!" said Tiny Tim, the last of all.

CHARLES DICKENS

29
Be Thankful

Christmas brings great gifts, from the presents people exchange to God's gift of Jesus Christ to the human family. When a gift is given, the receiver offers thanks. Take time to honor the gifts God has given you and thank him for his blessings in your life.

Praise God for the common, ordinary things, as well as for the special gifts the season brings. Sing praise songs as you vacuum and straighten the house. Count your blessings when you're driving to work or running errands. Be thankful for friends and family, for health and prosperity, and for saving grace. It is good to give thanks.

O our God, we thank you and
praise your glorious name!

1 CHRONICLES 29:13 NLT

Number a blank page from 1 to 100. Write down 100 things you are thankful for in your life.

Pure in Heart

Blessed are the pure in heart, for they shall see God.

MATTHEW 5:8 NKJV

Happy, happy Christmas, that can win us back to the delusions of our childhood days, recall to the old man the pleasures of his youth, and transport the traveler back to his own fireside and quiet home!

CHARLES DICKENS

30

Share Lots of Hugs

The door of the home swings wide open and loved ones greet you with a warm embrace. It's a beautiful picture that reminds you of how special the Christmas season can be. Yet many people feel lonely and left out during this season of happy family reunions. Let your empathetic embraces be a way of expanding the circle of love and encouragement.

Spread the love around and share lots of hugs. If you are filled with the joy of the season, share your joy with others. If you are feeling sad and lonely, seek out others who need encouragement, and you'll feel better, too.

Behold, how good and how pleasant it is for brethren to dwell together in unity!

PSALM 133:1 NKJV

 Embrace

Be the first one to reach out to others with a warm embrace. Let your heart lead and show you how to include shy people in the circle of love.

31

Create a *New* Tradition

Renew

As you enjoy favorite Christmas traditions, experiment by trying something different. Your celebration can embrace a mix of old and new.

Traditions bring depth and meaning to the Christmas celebration. But sometimes a tradition can lose its relevance or meaning in the face of life's changes. Creating a fresh tradition each year helps you welcome new delights along with old favorites.

It can be as simple as a new recipe for a festive dish or as complex as going somewhere different to celebrate the holidays. A new tradition can help you fill in the empty spaces when change or loss makes old traditions impossible. A new tradition lets you open your heart to the new things God wants to do in your life.

> There is something about saying, "We always do this," which helps keep the years together. Tradition is a good gift intended to guard the best gifts.

MADELEINE L'ENGLE

Eternal Love

Are you willing to believe that love
is the strongest thing in the world—
stronger than hate, stronger than evil,
stronger than death—and that the
blessed life which began in Bethlehem
nineteen hundred years ago is the
image and brightness of the Eternal
Love? Then you can keep Christmas.

HENRY VAN DYKE

32

Remember Christmas Past

Reminisce

Look through old photo albums together and share favorite stories of Christmases past over eggnog and cookies.

When Ebenezer Scrooge was visited by the Ghost of Christmas Past, he was reminded of happier times with friends and loved ones no longer living, but whose memories were still fresh in his heart. You don't need a ghost to remind you of treasured memories—all you need to do is take some time for remembering the joys of other Christmases.

Whether you are together with friends and family or reminiscing in a meditative moment alone, give thanks for the gifts God has brought through the years. Remembering the good things from Christmases past will help you appreciate the gifts that Christmas present offers you.

Remember his miracles and all his wonders and his fair decisions.

PSALM 105:5 CEV

33

*C*reate a *N*ativity *S*cene

Nativity scenes have been a Christmas favorite since Saint Francis created the first live Nativity scene in Assisi. The Madonna looks down on the baby in the straw and Joseph stands by, strong and proud. Shepherds hold lambs, wise men kneel, and oxen and donkeys look on. Angels hover and a star shines above.

Craftsmen and artists from many different cultures have created beautiful figures in a variety of materials. You can buy a wonderful Nativity scene to display year after year, or make your own. Your home Nativity scene can be a reminder of the drama and the beauty of that first Christmas.

> *The hinge of history is on the door of a Bethlehem stable.*
>
> RALPH W. SOCKMAN

Birth

Enjoy Nativity scenes from many lands. *The Night of the Child* offers photographs of the Upper Room Museum Nativity Collection and reflections written by Robert Benson.

34
Spend a Day at Home

Set aside a portion of your day for self-care. Take a long, luxurious bath, a healing nap, or do other body-nurturing activities that make you feel good.

🌰

The holiday season is packed with special events. Between Christmas errands and the regular round of daily duties, it's easy to overbook yourself. Prevent holiday burnout by choosing to spend a quiet day at home. Declare a personal holiday and make self-care a priority.

Instead of filling your at-home day with the usual chores and work, create an oasis of peace where you have some time to putter and dream. Make this a day for baking, decorating, or creative projects. Include time for spiritual renewal. A meditative walk, quiet time for spiritual reading, or communion with God in prayer will feed your spirit.

Home interprets heaven;
home is heaven for beginners.

CHARLES HENRY PARKHURST

The Face of God

God hides nothing. His very work
from beginning is revelation—a casting
aside of veil after veil, a showing unto
men of truth after truth. On and on
from fact divine he advances, until at
length in his son Jesus he unveils his
very face.

GEORGE MACDONALD

35

Adopt a Family

Share

Get a group of friends together to adopt a family and spread the giving between you.

Christmas is a time for giving and sharing. But for many families, it's a time of financial stress and hunger. Adopting a needy family is one way to ease the burdens of others and share the true spirit of the season.

Find out what each child in the family wants and needs. As well as gifts for the children, consider what is needed by the adults in the family. Create an extra goody basket filled with delicious delights that a poorer family could not afford. Decide whether or not to give anonymously. Charitable organizations offer wonderful ways to help a family or children.

> *Let's see how inventive we can be in encouraging love and helping out.*
>
> HEBREWS 10:24 MSG

36

Give the Gift of Time

One of your greatest treasures is your time. How you spend your time indicates where your priorities truly lie. If you say you love someone, but you have no time for them, then how are they to know you really care?

In this busy season, make a choice to give the gift of time. Take time to really be present when your friend wants to share her troubles. Slow down long enough to enjoy the companionship of loved ones. Give some time to church or charity. Give yourself the gift of a gentle hour of leisure. Spend some time alone with God in prayer.

What we weave in time we wear in eternity.

JOHN CHARLES RYLE

Presence

Instead of packing your schedule, leave room in your calendar for serendipity. Give God space and time to orchestrate divine encounters.

Christmas Wish

I wish you the joy of Christmas

The spirit's sweet repose,

I wish you the Peace of Christmas

To mark the old year's close;

I wish you the hope of Christmas

To cheer you on your way.

And a heart of faith and gladness

To face each coming day.

AUTHOR UNKNOWN

37

Share a Christmas Kiss

Mistletoe is renowned for its healing powers, partly because the plant continues to stay green even when the rest of the forest is clothed in winter snows. It became a medieval symbol of God's provision and grace. Families would often decorate doorways with sprigs of mistletoe as reminders of God's love, evolving into a tradition of lovers kissing under the mistletoe.

Hang mistletoe over a doorway and use it as a festive reason to share a loving Christmas kiss. You don't need this little evergreen plant to enjoy affectionate hugs and kisses, but a sprig of mistletoe is a happy reminder of a favorite Christmas tradition.

Hang up love's mistletoe over the earth and let us kiss under it all year round.

AUTHOR UNKNOWN

Kiss

Wear a sprig of mistletoe in your hat and encourage friends and loved ones to share a Christmas hug and kiss.

53

38

Be an Angel for a Day

Be an angel in your temperament, too. When someone crowds in front of you or acts rudely, smile and offer a silent prayer of blessing.

Christmas angels don't just decorate the tops of Christmas trees. They can be embodied in flesh and blood, too. You can be an angel for a day—or every day, if you want to.

Think of what angels are—and what they do. Angels are servants of God who bring messages of love and help mortals in this life. Now think of ways to imitate their service as you encounter others during your busy day. You can be an angel by looking for opportunities to share God's love with others through a friendly smile, a word of encouragement, or by offering a helping hand.

> *Angels are merely spirits sent to serve people who are going to be saved.*
>
> HEBREWS 1:14 CEV

Christmas Eve

The door is on the latch tonight,
The hearth-fire is aglow;
I seem to hear the passing feet—
The Christ Child in the snow.

My heart is open wide tonight,
For stranger, kith, or kin:
I would not bar a single door
Where love might enter in.

AUTHOR UNKNOWN

39

Enjoy a Cozy Fire

Warm

❧

Spend a quiet evening at home in front of the fire reading, writing in your journal, or wrapping presents.

❧

One of the greatest pleasures of winter is sitting in front of a fire in the fireplace, enjoying the warmth of the blaze, the crackling sound of sparks popping, and the marvelous scent of wood smoke as it rises up the chimney. Take time out to enjoy a cozy fire and dreamily watch the dancing flames.

Charles Dickens wrote about the Pickwick Club, a group of friends who would gather around a cheerful winter fire and enjoy merry company. Gather a few friends around your home fire for a festive time of laughter and good cheer. Offer eggnog and Christmas cookies as an extra treat.

The deep red blaze sent forth a rich glow that penetrated into the farthest corner of the room, and cast its cheerful tint on every face.

CHARLES DICKENS

40

Learn About Christmas Legends

One way to nurture closer relationships with family is to enjoy rituals and traditions together. Learning about Christmas legends and traditions will add to your enjoyment of the season and may give you ideas that you can adapt to your time and culture.

For example, Prince Albert brought the Christmas tree to England from Germany when he married Queen Victoria. Santa Claus evolved from legends built around a Christian bishop, Saint Nicholas, who lived in the fourth century A.D. There are many books available to introduce you to the meaning of favorite traditions and help you to adapt some for your own Christmas celebrations.

Tradition

Honor nurturing traditions this Christmas by celebrating a cherished yet neglected family tradition with loved ones.

> *For Christmas is tradition time*
> *Traditions that recall*
> *The precious memories down the years.*
>
> HELEN LOWRIE MARSHALL

His Coming

He comes to us as one unknown, without a name, as of old, by the lakeside he came to those men who knew him not. He speaks to us the same word, "Follow thou me!" and sets us to the tasks which he has to fulfill for our time. He commands. And to those who obey, whether they be wise or simple, he will reveal himself in the toils, the conflicts, the suffering which they shall pass through in his fellowship, and as an ineffable mystery, they shall learn in their own experience who he is.

ALBERT SCHWEITZER

41
Take Extra Time for Prayer

One way to keep spirits light during the holiday season is to take extra time for prayer. Spending time in God's presence will calm your spirit and remind you of why we celebrate Christmas.

Use Christmas traditions as a focus for prayer. Build prayer times around what you do each day. For example, before you go into the mall to shop, spend a few quiet minutes sitting in your car and praying. As you prepare to light candles on a cold evening, pause and make the lighting of each candle a prayer. Include God in your festivities and feel his love calm your heart.

Pause

🕊

Choose a Christmas or Advent devotional that will take you through each day of the season and use it as a reminder to pray.

🕊

Seek the LORD while you can find him. Call on him now while he is near.

ISAIAH 55:6 NLT

42

Be Patient and Kind

Kindness

The next time someone is rude or treats you thoughtlessly, offer a silent prayer of blessing to bring peace and God's love to the situation.

Traffic, crowds, and the pressure of piling seasonal celebrations on top of everyday priorities can make even the most serene person frustrated. Patience and kindness reflect God's forbearance and generosity and are especially needed during this season of brotherly love.

Be kind to people, even when they are not kind to you. Remember that people have their own struggles to deal with, and your kindness and patience can make life easier for everyone. Your calmness and care for others reflects God's loving care, too. Practicing patience is a gift you give yourself, as well as a gift you offer to those around you.

Be kind and compassionate to one another, forgiving each other, just as in Christ God forgave you.

EPHESIANS 4:32 NIV

43

Appreciate the Abundance

From brightly decorated shopping malls to exuberant light displays, Christmas is a time of abundance—and excess. Instead of becoming cynical in the face of a commercialized Christmas, look at and appreciate the abundance, even when it is expressed as tasteless excess.

Look more deeply into your own life for true abundance. Find pleasure in simple things that you often take for granted, whether it is a platter of cookies on the table or a pile of presents under the tree. Savor the delights of family and friends, health and home. Thank God for the abundance of love he gives you each and every day.

I have come that they may have life,
and have it to the full.

JOHN 10:10 NIV

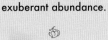

If you're tempted to criticize the excess of a modern commercial Christmas, choose instead to look at it as an expression of exuberant abundance.

61

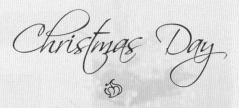

Christmas Day

I sometimes think we expect too much of Christmas Day. We try to crowd into it the long arrears of kindliness and humanity of the whole year. As for me, I like to take my Christmas a little at a time, all through the year. And thus I drift along into the holidays—let them overtake me unexpectedly—waking up some fine morning and suddenly saying to myself: "Why, this is Christmas Day!"

DAVID GRAYSON

44
Give the Gift of Music

One of the most beautiful gifts the season offers is the gift of music. Familiar Christmas carols blend with choral masterpieces like Handel's *Messiah*. Whether you choose the gorgeous tapestry of a classical orchestra or the toe-tapping jazziness of a modern singing group, you can share the gift of music with others.

Music lifts the spirit in ways that nothing else does. Take time to listen to music you love, especially the lovely music inspired by the meaning of Christ's birth. Put a favorite Christmas CD in someone's stocking or take a friend to a concert to share the joy of music that inspires you.

Music is the art of the prophets, the only art that can calm the agitations of the soul; it is one of the most magnificent and delightful presents God has given us.

MARTIN LUTHER

Listen

If you love to sing, offer your gift of music by joining a choir and taking part in a special Christmas performance.

45

Take Tea with a Friend

Relax

❄

For an extra treat, buy a new kind of tea to take home. And be sure to invite a friend over the next time you make a pot of tea.

❄

Make it a point to get together with friends. Even though everyone is busy, a simple teatime get-together offers an opportunity to catch up with one another's lives while taking a break from the Christmas rush.

Call a friend and set up a date for tea. Plan your Christmas shopping around a friendly tea break. You can meet over a hot cup of Earl Grey or jasmine tea at your favorite tea shop or restaurant. Take time to talk about the things that are important to you and share what's been happening in your lives. Enjoy the pleasure of one another's company.

Friends are the sunshine of life.

JOHN HAY

True Hearts

Blessed is the influence of one true,
loving soul on another.

GEORGE ELIOT

Remember, the greatest gift is not
found in a store or under a tree, but in
the hearts of true friends.

CINDY LEW

46

Forgo Formality

Easy

❦

Enjoy a more intimate and informal prayer relationship with God. Include him in your everyday activities as well as more formal worship occasions.

❦

A table gleaming with crystal and silver, a formal dress and suit—extravagant holiday arrangements can be exciting and brilliant. But sometimes living up to sparkling magazine layouts of expensive parties is too much work for busy people. If you want to invest more time in enjoying friends than in elaborate preparations, create a more casual celebration.

Encourage lightness of spirit and spontaneity by forgoing formality. Casual entertaining can help you concentrate more on matters of the heart than on impressing others. A less formal approach helps others feel comfortable, opening the way for more intimate confidences in a relaxed atmosphere.

Make it clear. Make it simple. Emphasize the essentials. Forget about impressing.

CHARLES SWINDOLL

47

Savor Favorite Foods

'Tis the season for feasting and festive foods. It's time to pull out the Christmas recipe file and make the family favorites that are traditional to the seasonal table. Once-a-year cookies and fudge make the holidays memorably delicious. Savor the Christmas Day feast of roast beef or turkey and all the fixings, as well as the conversational feast around the table.

Be thankful for the bountiful feast and the wide variety of foods that are available to you in these days of well-stocked grocery stores. If you like to cook, offer a special feast for friends and family that is served with love and blessing.

For those who love it, cooking is at once child's play and adult joy. And cooking done with care is an act of love.

CRAIG CLAIBORNE

Enhance the flavor of the feasts with gratitude. Offer thanks for the bounteous blessings and thank God that you have food on the table.

Delicious

It's fun to get together and have something good to eat at least once a day. That's what human life is all about— enjoying things.

JULIA CHILD

My kitchen is a mystical place, a kind of temple for me. It is a place where the surfaces seem to have significance, where the sounds and odors carry meaning that transfers from the past and bridges to the future.

PEARL BAILEY

48

Fast for a Day

Fasting is more than mere self-denial. It's about allowing your body to rest and renew itself while taking a refreshing spiritual break. The stomach needs some time to clear itself out, and a brief fast can help you recover from holiday overindulgence. A juice fast or just eating fresh fruits and vegetables can help cleanse your system. Don't forget to drink plenty of water.

As you give your body a cleansing rest by fasting for a meal or two, give your spirit a rest by spending quiet time in prayer and meditation. You'll be refreshed and better able to enjoy the holidays.

> *The best of all medicines are resting and fasting.*
>
> BENJAMIN FRANKLIN

Recover

If you indulge in rich foods and Christmas desserts one day, eat only fresh fruits and vegetables and homemade broth for a day or two after.

49

Use Fresh Herbs for Decorating

Scent

Buy or make a wreath made of fresh culinary herbs. As it dries out you can hang it in the kitchen and use the herbs for seasoning food through the winter.

Herbs have been grown for centuries for healing and culinary use. Useful culinary and medicinal herbs and aromatic plants bring pleasure and healing into your home, whether you enjoy a large herb garden or just a few pots on the windowsill.

Herbs are living links with the past. From the monastery garden where herbs were grown for healing to Victorian gardens of the nineteenth century where each herb had a spiritual or allegorical meaning, fresh herbs have been used for medicine, food, and fragrant delight. Aromatic plants and fresh herbs can sweeten the air of your home and make it a paradise of garden beauty.

> *Rosemary was once a central plant in the Christmas celebration. . . . Swags of rosemary hung beside the holly and ivy, scenting the air with its aromatic oils.*

> MAUREEN GILMER

Seeds of Love

Seeds of kindness, goodwill, and human understanding, planted in fertile soil, spring up into deathless friendships, big deeds of worth, and a memory that will not soon fade out.

GEORGE MATTHEW ADAMS

How many observe Christ's birthday! How few, his precepts! O! 'tis easier to keep holidays than commandments.

BENJAMIN FRANKLIN

50

Gather Together with Loved Ones

Gather together with others and enjoy a celebratory meal. Dress up and make it an occasion to remember.

Gathering together with friends and family is a holiday tradition. Whether you are toasting the splendors of the season at a party with friends or nestled near the home fires on Christmas Eve, don't let the season go by without telling loved ones how much they mean to you.

Even if you are alone this year, there are ways to celebrate the love of those you miss. Call friends and family who are far away. Send cards, letters, and gifts. And for those who are no longer in this life, lift your sorrows to God and treasure the memories you hold in your heart.

Most of all, love each other as if your life depended on it. Love makes up for practically anything.

1 PETER 4:8 MSG

51

Celebrate the Moment

Make every moment count. Cultivate an awareness of the splendors hidden in the ordinary moments as well as the special ones. Happy times are often fleeting and far between, and it's easy to live in anticipation of a future pleasure that comes and goes far too fast.

Spread the pleasure out by cultivating an attitude that celebrates each moment, no matter what the moment brings. Doing dishes can be a celebration of soap, warm water, and gratitude; getting a work project finished is a reason to celebrate; and the person smiling across the table at you is all the party you need right now.

At Christmas play and make good cheer,
For Christmas comes but once a year.

THOMAS TUSSER

Now

Make a contract with yourself to stay focused in the moment instead of worrying about the future or going over the past.

Blessings

Somehow, not only for Christmas,

But all the long year through,

The joy that you give to others,

Is the joy that comes back to you.

And the more you spend in blessing,

The poor and lonely and sad,

The more of your heart's possessing,

Returns to you glad.

JOHN GREENLEAF WHITTIER

52

Give Your Best

You'll have no regrets when you give your best—whether it's your best effort on a project or buying the best gift for someone you love. You may not be able to do things perfectly or give expensive and rare gifts. But when you give the best you have to offer, God blesses what you give and multiplies it.

God gave us his very best when he sent his Son. That gift frees you to offer your best to life because God is always with you, always strengthening you, and always encouraging you to be the very best he created you to be.

Whatever is good and perfect comes down to us from God our Father, who created all the lights in the heavens.

JAMES 1:17 NLT

Generosity

The next time you're tempted to settle for second-best, think about what it feels like to enjoy the very best. Now do the best you can in this moment.

53

Stick to Your Budget

Discipline

Be sure to include a budget for charitable giving. From planned tithes to special offerings, budgets that contribute generously to the greater good are blessed by God.

Extravagance is easy when the entire world goes on a Christmas buying spree. Before you splurge on another extra, ask yourself if this is the best use of your money. Budgets can help you honor spiritual priorities in the way you spend your money.

Create a Christmas spending plan. Make a budget and stick to it. Be realistic and plan for impulse spending instead of trying to control every penny. When you go over budget in one area, cut back in another. Sticking to your budget, especially when it comes to using credit cards, will keep you from experiencing after-holiday regrets as bills come due.

Don't gamble on the pot of gold at the end of the rainbow, hocking your house against a lucky chance.

PROVERBS 22:26 MSG

54
Enjoy the Music of Silence

Turn off the TV and radio. Take a break from the holiday frenzy and drink in the sounds of blessed silence. Make this Christmas a time to listen. God can then speak to you, and you'll hear his still, small voice in the silence of your heart.

If you can't create an oasis of silence in your home, go where you can find healing silence. Find a quiet church or sanctuary. Walk in the woods or experience a silent night under a starry sky. Make room in your life for silence, and its melody will sing to your heart.

> *Silence is more musical*
> *than any song.*
>
> CHRISTINA ROSSETTI

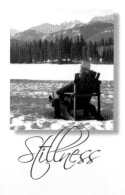

Stillness

Take ten minutes in the midst of a busy day for silent reflection. Take a walk in a quiet garden, forest, or park.

Prayerful Attentiveness

Silence is a positive kind of hearing, which requires turning off the knob that tunes in to active, literal life and tuning on the one that amplifies the movements of the soul.

THOMAS MOORE

The whole thing boils down to giving ourselves in prayer a chance to realize that we have what we seek. We don't have to rush after it. It is there all the time, and if we give it time, it will make itself known to us.

THOMAS MERTON

55

Remember Those Who Are Sad

Life doesn't stop for the holidays. And neither does illness, death, or sorrow. Grief can feel overwhelming in a time when everyone else seems to be rejoicing. If someone you know is going through a difficult time, let them know you care about their sorrow and offer to help in any way you are able.

Remember in prayer all those who grieve, who are lonely, and who feel sad. Your heartfelt prayer, whether it's for people you know or for those suffering around the globe, does make a difference. Be it a prayer, a hand reaching out, or a monetary gift, your compassion helps comfort the sorrowful.

Do not let us fail one another in interest, care, and practical help; but supremely we must not fail one another in prayer.

MICHAEL BAUGHEN

Comfort

Include a note in a Christmas card and let a friend know that you are praying for him or her in this time of sadness.

56

Find the Perfect Gift

Choose

🌸

Give something that enhances a loved one's favorite hobby or interest: a sketch pad for an artist, a trowel and seeds for a gardener, a biography for a history buff.

One of the greatest joys in giving is knowing that the gift is perfect for the one who is receiving it. "Oh! It's just what I wanted!" and a smiling face tell you that this gift will be appreciated long after Christmas has come and gone. Make an extra effort to find gifts that people will use and enjoy. Think about the hobbies and interests of each person you are shopping for.

Also remember that God has delivered perfect gifts to you: loved ones, health, satisfying work, home pleasures. And the best gift of all is the Christ child born in Bethlehem two thousand years ago.

If [your child] asks for fish, do you scare him with a live snake on his plate? As bad as you are, you wouldn't think of such a thing. You're at least decent to your own children. So don't you think the God who conceived you in love will be even better?

MATTHEW 7:10–11 MSG

Think on These Things

Christmas is not a time or a season but a state of mind. To cherish peace and good will, to be plenteous in mercy, is to have the real spirit of Christmas. If we think on these things, there will be born in us a Savior and over us will shine a star sending its gleam of hope to the world.

CALVIN COOLIDGE

57

Let Love Rule in Your Heart

Love

Recognize that God blesses the world through our loving actions. Reach out and be a blessing to someone today.

Love is a great beautifier. It makes every plain face fairer and every fair face beautiful. When you look at others with love, you see beyond their faults and foibles straight into the heart. Let love rule in your heart, and you will discover a more joyous and blessed experience during the holidays.

Love more creatively this Christmas by seeing the greatness within each person, no matter how unlikely it seems by surface appearances. Loving others means that you want the best for them and are willing to do something to help make that happen in their lives. Loving others is another way to love God.

Love seeks one thing only: the good of the one loved. It leaves all other secondary effects to take care of themselves.

THOMAS MERTON

58

Have a Christmas Movie Night

Pull up a comfortable chair. Pop some popcorn, and grab something cold to drink. Then sit back and enjoy a stack of Christmas movies. You may enjoy old favorites such as *It's a Wonderful Life*, *White Christmas*, or *Miracle on 34th Street*. A modern Christmas drama or a silly holiday comedy may be what you're in the mood for.

Planning a movie night can help you ration your TV viewing; when you know you have a movie night to look forward to, you're less likely to sit and channel surf beforehand. So gather friends and family and enjoy one night of being couch potatoes.

Christmas waves a magic wand over this world, and behold, everything is softer and more beautiful.

NORMAN VINCENT PEALE

Escape

Buy some snacks, bring out the Christmas cookies, and make some hot cider for watching. Don't forget a few healthy "veggie munchies" as well.

Simplicity

May each Christmas, as it comes, find us more and more like Him who at this time became a little child, for our sake, more simple-minded, more humble, more affectionate, more resigned, more happy, more full of God.

JOHN HENRY NEWMAN

It's easy to be clever. But the really clever thing is to be simple.

JULE STYNE

59

Beat the Holiday Blues

Though the Christmas season is filled with joyous celebration, the holiday blues can make life miserable. If you want to beat the holiday blues, make plans to head them off before they start.

Take care of yourself. Get plenty of sleep and regular exercise. If you're tired, you'll be more prone to falling into depression. Eat well instead of grabbing fast food. Temper your expectations of yourself and of the holiday. Plan to take retreats away from the rush of seasonal activities. When you're feeling overextended, cut back on activities and take time to nurture yourself. Ask God for wisdom to cope with emotional lows.

> *He heals the brokenhearted and bandages their wounds.*
>
> PSALM 147:3 NLT

Nurture

Put on some up-tempo music and enjoy a few minutes of musical celebration. Move your body and sing along; you'll be energized by the joyful sound.

60
Make Your Home Fragrant

Aroma

❧

Buy flowering plants to add beauty and scent to your home: stately lilies, charming paperwhite narcissus, glorious amaryllis, or delicately sensuous jasmine.

❧

Fragrance takes you back in time, transporting you instantly to holidays long ago. The scent of your mother's perfume or the smell of a favorite dish simmering on the stove can evoke your childhood with one fleeting impression. Create a welcoming holiday home through the magic of fragrance.

Freshly baked bread, apples and cinnamon, gingerbread cookies, or a nourishing pot of soup creates delicious kitchen odors. The wreath that greets you at the door smells of fresh evergreen. Potpourri in a bowl breathes out a fragrance that fills the room with soft scent. There are many ways to make your home fragrant for the holidays.

> *In Hebrew . . . the word for "spirit" is* Ruach *and for "scent" is* Reach. *This reflects the ancient belief that sanctity is characterized by divine fragrance.*

> Dr. Naomie Poran

Innocent Wisdom

Most sensible people say that adults cannot be expected to appreciate Christmas as much as children appreciate it. . . . But I am not sure that even sensible people are always right. . . . I enjoy Christmas more than I did when I was a child. My faith demands that such be the case. The more mature I become, the more I need to be but a child.

G. K. CHESTERTON

61

Enjoy a Daily Bible Reading

Scripture

The Book of Common Prayer offers readings for each day of the year and each Sunday. Advent devotionals also take you through seasonal readings.

One way to meditate on the true meaning of Christmas is to read the Bible every day. Set aside at least fifteen minutes for reading and meditation. Use a modern Bible translation for easy comprehension, and a Bible commentary or handbook will give you more background for better understanding.

Christmas begins with Christ, so start with the stories in Matthew and Luke that tell about the first Christmas and the events leading up to it. Delve into the Gospels to read the story of Christ's life. If you're unfamiliar with the Bible, a good place to begin is the Gospel of John.

Those who discover these words live, really live;
body and soul, they're bursting with health.

PROVERBS 4:22 MSG

62

Lighten Up

This is a season of joyous celebration. It's a time to rekindle childlike wonder and delight. If you have been feeling a bit too serious lately, decide that Christmas is the perfect excuse to lighten up.

Let the simple pleasures of the Christmas season remind you of how much good there is in life. Get together with friends who make you laugh. Cultivate a happier mood by keeping a sense of perspective. Remember that most of the things you worry about today will be forgotten tomorrow. Take your troubles to God in prayer and leave them there so you can celebrate with a lighter heart.

Humor is the prelude to faith, and laughter is the beginning of prayer.

REINHOLD NIEBUHR

Smile

Play with children—your own or someone else's. Revel in their simple pleasure and join in their laughter.

63
*C*ultivate a *P*eaceful *H*eart

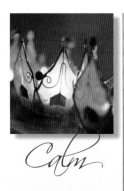

🌢

Carry a card bearing a quote or Bible verse to remind you that God's peace and comfort are available wherever you are.

🌢

Crowded malls, holiday traffic, and long lists of things to do can steal your peace of mind and heart. But when the holiday rush leaves you frazzled and breathless, you can choose peace. Ask God to help you cultivate a peaceful heart that is not moved by the swirling activities all around.

You can find quietness within your own heart. When you are calm and focused, you are peaceful even during the holiday frenzy. Let God be your oasis of peace—whether you are in a candlelit cathedral listening to a Christmas oratorio or in the middle of the mall watching all the people rush by.

The holy LORD God of Israel had told all of you,
"I will keep you safe if you turn back to
me and calm down. I will make you
strong if you quietly trust me."

ISAIAH 30:15 CEV

The Power of Love

We never live so intensely as when we love strongly. We never realize ourselves so vividly as when we are in the full glow of love for others.

WALTER RAUSCHENBUSCH

The day will come when, after harnessing space, the winds, the tides, and gravitation, we shall harness for God the energies of love. And on that day, for the second time in the history of the world, man will have discovered fire.

PIERRE TEILHARD DE CHARDIN

64

*M*ake a *C*hristmas *B*asket

Create

Create a themed gift basket (Italian dinner, garden teatime, bath delights) with someone special in mind. Wrap it beautifully and give it to them.

Christmas baskets come in all shapes and sizes. From a tiny basket filled with bath treats for a friend to a generous basket bursting with everything a family needs to make Christmas merry, the variety and themes are as limitless as your imagination.

Fill your Christmas basket with the needs of the recipients in mind. If you're buying for a family, include age-appropriate toys and clothing. Love is expressed in thoughtful choices. Use your creative imagination to fill the basket with good things that you know people will love to use and enjoy. Your basket will remind others that God loves them.

Be kind. Remember that everyone you meet is fighting a hard battle.

HARRY THOMPSON

65

Donate in Someone's Name

Sometimes the best Christmas gift is a donation in someone's name. You may offer a charitable donation to honor a friend or loved one. You can also give an anonymous gift in the name of Jesus.

Consider this anonymous mid-December gift idea: Surprise a struggling family by going into your local department store and making a payment on (or paying off) their layaway—one that includes toys. Say your generosity is a Christmas present from Jesus. Imagine the pleasure of a parent showing up to make a payment and being told that the account is paid and they can take the toys home.

> *You do not have to be rich to be generous.*
> *If he has the spirit of true generosity,*
> *a pauper can give like a prince.*
>
> CORRINE U. WELLS

Give

Go to a dollar store and buy several inexpensive, old-fashioned fun presents—modeling clay, jacks, games, balsa-wood airplanes, puzzles—and donate them to a family or a children's charity.

Look for God

We wait in the hope that when the moment comes, we will, like the shepherds, have the presence of mind to hear the heavenly host and the spirit to head off to Bethlehem to see this thing which has come to pass.

ROBERT BENSON

If Christmas is about anything, it's about a baby—God's baby, born in a stable, who changed the world forever. When we come to the stables in our lives, let us be wise and remember to look for God.

JOHN MAXWELL

66

God So Loved the World . . .

Christ is the expression of God's love for humanity, and his story has inspired and comforted believers for more than two thousand years. Remembering the love of God expressed through the life of Christ will enrich your understanding of the mysterious ways God works in the world.

One simple way to know more about Jesus Christ is to read his words and meditate on them. The Beatitudes from the Sermon on the Mount (Matthew 5:3–10) and Jesus' conversation with Nicodemus (John 3:1–21) are good places to begin. Take a moment to reflect on the meaning of Christ's birth. Remember that Christmas is celebrated because God loves all of humanity.

God so loved the world that He gave His only begotten Son, that whoever believes in Him should not perish but have everlasting life.

JOHN 3:16 NKJV

Meaning

Read through the Gospel of John in a modern Bible translation. This book of the Bible offers a wonderful introduction to the life of Christ.

95

67

Put an Angel on Your Tree

❧

Buy or collect feathers to hang on the tree, just as if an angel had shed a feather or two as she was passing by. Dust feathers with glitter and tie with a ribbon.

❧

The word *angel* comes from the biblical word for "messenger" and "evangelism." It means "the one who brings a good word." Angels bring messages of hope. You can celebrate the message the angels brought by putting an angel on your tree. Some people like to top the tree with an angel, while others love to hang angels in the evergreen branches.

Angels sang of God's glory on the night Jesus was born. They spoke to prophets and guided God's children during times of trouble. When you look at the angel that decorates your tree, remember that God sends angels to remind you of his love.

The angels are the dispensers and administrators of the divine beneficence toward us; they regard our safety, undertake our defense, direct our ways, and exercise a consistent solicitude that no evil befalls us.

The House Beautiful

The Beauty of the house is Order.

The Blessing of the house is Contentment.

The Glory of the house is Hospitality.

The Crown of the house is Godliness.

AUTHOR UNKNOWN

68
Say Grace

Gratitude

🍂

Go around the table
and have each person
offer thanks for
the best thing that
happened during
the day.

🍂

The old-fashioned habit of saying grace offers a simple way of pausing and gratefully remembering the gifts God bestows. It doesn't matter what you say, but that you pause and take the time to give thanks. Saying grace before meals makes the mundane more meaningful.

One way to introduce the ritual of grace to your family circle is to write your own personal prayer. There are books of prayers and poems available, too, such as June Cotner's book *Christmas Blessings*. You can also incorporate spontaneous thanks for the events of the day. Life feels far richer when you take the time to offer gratitude with grace before meals.

We say grace before our meals—not to make our
food holy, but to acknowledge gratefully
that it is already holy.

WILLIAM MCNAMARA

69

Keep a Cheerful Attitude

You'd think that a happy holiday would make it easy to stay cheerful. But people register their highest levels of depression during the Christmas season. Between short days and long lists of things to do, you have to decide to cultivate a cheerful attitude.

One way to stay positive even when negative things happen is to step back from stressful situations, giving yourself time to regain perspective. Another is to take good care of yourself. Then you'll have energy for cheerfulness. Let prayer reconnect you to a sense of God's presence so you can see that everything is a blessing, even when it's in disguise.

A cheerful disposition is good for your health; gloom and doom leave you bone-tired.

PROVERBS 17:22 MSG

Perspective

Take a brisk walk outdoors. Don't forget that daily exercise energizes you and raises your spirits.

Gratitude

Thou hast given so much to me,
Give one thing more—a grateful heart;
Not thankful when it pleaseth me,
As if thy blessings had spare days;
But such a heart, whose pulse may be
Thy praise.

GEORGE HERBERT

70

Make an Advent Wreath

There are four Sundays in Advent. One of the treasured rituals of this church season is to create an Advent wreath with four candles—three purple and one pink—each representing a different aspect of the coming of Christ. Each Sunday another candle is lit until all four candles glow on the last Sunday before Christmas.

Set the candles in a circle of evergreens and enjoy the ceremony of lighting the Advent candles. The first candle represents God's promises (hope), the second God's law (love), the third the prophets who herald God's coming (joy), and the fourth the coming of the light of Christ into a dark world (peace).

Advent. The coming of quiet joy. Arrival of radiant light in our darkness.

AUTHOR UNKNOWN

Advent

As you light the Advent candles, read an appropriate portion of Scripture aloud. Advent resources offer suggested verses, carols, and readings.

71

Take Candid Photos

Picture

Bring a disposable camera and gift certificate for developing the film to a friend's party. Have everyone take plenty of candid photos!

One of the delights of Christmas is seeing friends and loved ones. Taking plenty of candid photos at parties and gatherings will help you extend the celebration and remember these joyous reunions for a lifetime. Catching people at a moment of unself-conscious fun offers a simple way to remember them at their best.

In these days of digital cameras, candid photos can be put on computer disk and shared easily through e-mail. Of course, any camera will take a candid picture, if the person behind the camera is ready for that perfect instant when laughter and love shine from friendly faces.

Look at everything as though you were seeing it either for the first or last time. Then your time on earth will be filled with glory.

BETTY SMITH

Homecoming

The happiest holidays are those people go home for. Home is where no unkind word is spoken, and where the good smells from the kitchen tell of deep affection. The tree is lighted and waiting. The old folks are at the door, their faces beaming with pure welcome. The laughter comes closer than that of other days to the laughter of the angels.

AUTHOR UNKNOWN

72

Entertain Strangers and Angels

Invite those who might be alone at Christmas to share your Christmas dinner. Ask someone you don't know well out for tea and talk.

You could be entertaining angels this Christmas. Whether they are angelic messengers with wings or human beings who are the angels in your life, everyone is welcomed into the circle of love by your openness of heart and hospitable spirit. When you open your home and welcome strangers as well as friends, you are entertaining angels no matter what their disguise.

When you host a party or get-together, make sure that everyone feels welcome. Introduce people to one another and make sure that new people are included in the group activities. Honor each guest with your best, and you will honor God.

Be sure to welcome strangers into your home. By doing this, some people have welcomed angels as guests, without even knowing it.

HEBREWS 13:2 CEV

73

Attend Christmas Eve Services

The season of expectation in Advent unfolds into the season of jubilant celebration at the arrival of the Christ on Christmas Eve. Churches offer beautiful candlelight services on Christmas Eve, and going to services is the perfect way for the family to experience the mystery and wonder of Christmas.

Plan to attend Christmas Eve services at a church near you. Join in singing the familiar carols, listen to the story of Christ's birth, and enjoy the lovely atmosphere. Meditate on the meaning of Christmas. Then go home to a delicious homemade supper before snuggling under the covers in anticipation of Christmas morning.

Come, and behold him, born the King of angels;
O come, let us adore him . . . Christ the Lord!

JOHN FRANCIS WADE,
TRANS. FREDERICK OAKELEY

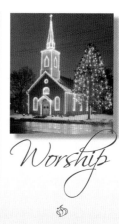

Worship

On Christmas Eve,
turn down the lights
and give each family
member a candle
to light. Have each
person share a
holiday memory as
the candles are lit.

105

74

Deck the Halls with Evergreens

Decorate

Drape tiny white twinkle lights around inside windows and over the mantel. Weave lights among evergreens and ornaments to highlight arrangements.

Whether you go on an expedition into the great outdoors or take a trip to your local florist, decorating with fresh greens offers a simple and inexpensive way to make your home more festive. Bring in armfuls of fragrant evergreens and deck the halls to your heart's delight. Invite others over to trim the tree and deck the halls, too.

Intersperse evergreen arrangements with ornaments and candles. Use them in floral arrangements. From a swag hung over the mantel to a green wreath and red bow on your front door, fresh evergreens are a reminder that God's love is ever green in your heart as well.

Now, the tree is decorated with bright merriment, and song, and dance, and cheerfulness. And they are welcome. Innocent and welcome be they ever held, beneath the branches of the Christmas Tree, which cast no gloomy shadow!

CHARLES DICKENS

Christmas Treasure

The earth has grown old
with its burden of care,
But at Christmas
it always is young;
The heart of the jewel
burns lustrous and fair,
And its soul full of music
breaks forth on the air,
When the song of angels
is sung.

PHILLIPS BROOKS

75

Take It as It Comes

Surrender

You make plans to celebrate the holidays and then something comes up—a flat tire, a canceled event, an unexpected illness. When plans change unexpectedly, you can allow frustration to rob you of your holiday joy, or you can choose to trust that everything, even the delays and detours, is in divine order.

Being prepared is a great way to enjoy the "now." Shop early for unexpected events like illnesses, extra guests, or pressure at work.

Take life as it comes, and you'll weather its tempests more easily. Colds and flu may make you take a much-needed time of rest. Plans gone awry often make room for pleasant surprises. Life happens; go with the flow, and let God show you how to enjoy whatever comes.

May the God of hope fill you with all joy and peace as you trust in him, so that you may overflow with hope by the power of the Holy Spirit.

ROMANS 15:13 NIV

76

*C*herish the *M*emories

Every Christmas offers its own precious memories. From baby's first Christmas to Grandfather's last year with the family, you'll want to make sure that you don't miss those fleeting moments with the ones you love. Make the most of these special times by choosing to live fully in the moment.

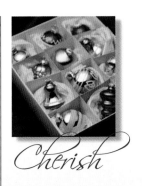

*C*herish

Pay attention to the here and now. Look at each person in the circle of love as if you're seeing them for the first time. Take photos, write in your journal, create a memory book to pass on to future generations. Thank God for the gifts of love expressed through family and friends.

Wrap a family heirloom and pass it on to your children so they can enjoy Great-grandmother's coin spoons or Grandfather's wood-working tools.

If you let yourself be absorbed completely, if you surrender completely to the moments as they pass, you live more richly those moments.

ANNE MORROW LINDBERGH

The Holy Land

We saunter toward the Holy Land, till one day the sun shall shine more brightly than ever he has done, shall perchance shine into our minds and hearts, and light up our whole lives with a great awakening light, as warm and serene and golden as on a bank-side in autumn.

HENRY DAVID THOREAU

77

Give the Gift of Encouragement

One of the greatest gifts you can give another human being is the gift of seeing his or her inner greatness. In a world that criticizes and discourages, the gift of encouragement offers a statement of faith in another person's potential, and an affirmation of each human being's worth in God's eyes.

Tell your young nephew that he catches the ball like a pro. Let your friend know that you believe in her dreams. Write a note of love and appreciation to your beloved. Applaud generously, praise often. Encourage others in their dreams and you will find the courage to pursue your own dreams.

> *The really great man is the man who makes every man feel great.*
>
> G. K. Chesterton

Write a letter on decorative paper to your loved ones, noting their personal growth through the year. List what you are grateful for about them.

78

Be Creative

Imagine

❧

Purchase a wreath, some ribbon, and a few ornaments from your local hobby store. With a hot glue gun and some creativity, you can produce the perfect gift for a coworker or best friend in just minutes.

❧

You are born creative. You don't have to be labeled "officially" creative—as an artist, performer, or inventor—to express yourself in creative ways. You do it naturally, just by being you. Let Christmas give you more reasons to express yourself creatively.

Try a new dish, make a wreath, or pull out the camera and take some pictures of winter scenes. Go to a crafts store and browse the aisles till you find the perfect Christmas project that will stretch your creative boundaries. Most of all, remember that the life you live is a creative gift you can offer to God with all the love that's within you.

We are His workmanship, created in Christ Jesus for good works, which God prepared beforehand that we should walk in them.

EPHESIANS 2:10 NKJV

Forever Young

After all, Christmas is but a big love affair to remove the wrinkles of the year with kindly remembrances.

JOHN WANAMAKER

The pursuit of truth and beauty is a sphere of activity in which we are permitted to remain children all our lives.

ALBERT EINSTEIN

79
Practice Forgiveness

Forgive

Write down on a sheet of paper the name of anyone you harbor anger toward. Pray for that person, then burn the paper as a sign of willingness to let your anger go.

Christmastime speaks of goodwill and peace. It's a wonderful time to practice forgiveness. As Christ chose to forgive others, so you can imitate Christ by forgiving those who hurt you. Give forgiveness to others, and ask God to forgive you for the things you have done and the things you have left undone.

Forgiving others—and yourself—creates an oasis of grace in your life. You'll discover that you have more energy for positive choices because you're not draining your energy away in negative attitudes. Forgiveness—or at least the willingness to forgive—can release God's energizing love in your life.

Smart people know how to hold their tongue; their grandeur is to forgive and forget.

PROVERBS 19:11 MSG

80
Enjoy a Holiday Fiesta

From a Swedish Saint Lucia breakfast to a German Christmas tree, Christmas is celebrated all around the world. Explore holiday traditions from different cultures and adapt them to your own Christmas celebrations.

For example, the Mexican culture celebrates the Nativity of Christ and the events leading up to it. Children dress up as Joseph and Mary, knocking on neighborhood doors, asking if there is room for Christ in the hearts and homes of those who dwell there. Adapt these colorful customs and make your own holiday fiesta with a living Nativity scene, a brilliant piñata, and delicious Mexican dishes. Make your home a place that welcomes the Christ child.

It isn't the big pleasures that count the most: it's making a great deal out of the little ones.

JEAN WEBSTER

Party

Hang a piñata, play salsa and Latin American music, and read a Mexican Christmas story to enjoy a "South of the Border" evening.

Incarnation

The Incarnation, which is for popular Christianity synonymous with the historical birth and earthly life of Christ, is for the mystic not only this but also a perpetual Cosmic and personal process. It is an everlasting bringing forth, in the universe and also in the individual and ascending soul, of the divine and perfect Life, the pure character of God.

EVELYN UNDERHILL

81

Give Something Green and Growing

Give a gift that keeps on giving long after the holidays have passed. Give something green and growing. A pot of primroses, a living Christmas tree, a gorgeous house-plant, or even a gardening book and some packets of seeds are all reminders that winter does not last forever, and spring's lovely greenery and blossoms will come in God's good season.

Choosing something that grows is a cele-bration of life. Nothing makes a more cheerful decoration or thoughtful gift than a pot of bulbs that bloom in the winter or a lush green plant that will give pleasure all year round.

Bloom

Create a personalized pot of paperwhite narcissus. Choose an interesting container and colorful glass or stones. Tie the gift with a bright ribbon.

Of all the gifts I have each year,
some sparkling, bright and glowing,
I think the gifts I hold most dear
are ones so green and growing.

AUTHOR UNKNOWN

82

Feed the Birds and Beasts

Nourish

String popcorn, nuts, and fresh cranberries and decorate an outdoor tree for the birds. Enjoy watching the birds flock to their new favorite tree.

Remember God's creatures at this time of year, too. Make sure pets are kept warm and fed well. Buy a Christmas chew toy for Fido or a special treat for Kitty. When you remember to take care of the animals, you are participating with God in providing for them.

Toss apples out for the deer, nuts for squirrels. Put up a birdhouse and scatter birdseed, then watch the winged show. Christmas bounty can be extended to all creatures, including the four-legged and furry ones.

Look at the birds of the air; they do not sow or reap or store away in barns, and yet your heavenly Father feeds them.

MATTHEW 6:26 NIV

83

Collect and Share Family Recipes

Almost everyone has a favorite Christmas recipe they take pride in. Whether you find a great cookie recipe at your neighbor's open house or a wonderful potluck classic in Grandmother's recipe file, you can enrich your repertoire of holiday specialties by collecting and sharing favorite recipes.

Homemade food makes a fun and inexpensive gift, so cook up an extra batch of family favorites to share with others. Have a recipe exchange party to which each person brings a dish and the recipe to share. Pass on family recipes to the younger generation. And remember, loving hands and grateful hearts make any dish more delicious.

Food, like a loving touch or a glimpse of divine power, has that ability to comfort.

NORMAN KOLPAS

Savor

Cook an extra batch
of cookies or a
favorite family dish to
share with a friend or
neighbor. Attach the
recipe on a
recipe card.

Back Home Again

Smell is a potent wizard that transports us across thousands of miles and all the years we have lived.

HELEN KELLER

This is the true nature of home—it is the place of peace; the shelter, not only from injury, but from all terror, doubt, and division.

JOHN RUSKIN

84
*M*ake a *G*ingerbread *H*ouse

Gingerbread has been a favorite Christmas treat for centuries. Fourteenth-century Germans took gingerbread so seriously that they formed guilds of gingerbread artisans. They made elaborate gingerbread castles and architectural wonders for the aristocracy. The Brothers Grimm introduced Hansel and Gretel's gingerbread house, and gingerbread treats migrated to America with German immigrants.

Creating a gingerbread house can be a family activity or a creative project for your artist's heart. If you want to create something different, try making a gingerbread ark, complete with animals. As you build and decorate, meditate on the ways loving hands have built the home that shelters you.

Through wisdom a house is built, and by understanding it is established; by knowledge the rooms are filled with all precious and pleasant riches.

PROVERBS 24:3–4 NKJV

Build

Decorate gingerbread men and hang them on the Christmas tree as edible ornaments.

85
Hold a Gift Exchange

Exchange

☙

Instead of a gift, have each person bring one ornament. Number the ornaments, then have each guest draw a number and receive the ornament with the corresponding number.

When you have a large group of friends and a small budget, make things easier by holding a gift exchange. Instead of giving something to everyone, decide to draw names and then give only to one person. Name a comfortable price range so that everyone feels they can afford to give and to keep from escalating costs (and creating possible hurt feelings) with competitive giving.

Lighten things up even further and have a White Elephant gift exchange. Everyone can wrap one no-longer-needed item—preferably something amusing—and let each person choose an intriguing package to unwrap. Enjoy the lighthearted fun.

Celebrate the happiness that friends are always giving. make every day a holiday and celebrate just living!

AMANDA BRADLEY

Glad Hearts

Life is short and we have never too much time for gladdening the hearts of those who are traveling the dark journey with us. Oh be swift to love, make haste to be kind.

HENRI FREDERIC AMIEL

Laughter is the sun that drives winter from the human face.

VICTOR HUGO

86

Spread Love and Laughter

✍

Make a simple
recording of you
reading your favorite
Christmas stories and
poems to send to a
faraway friend or
loved one.

✍

It's the simple gestures that mean the most. Many people are heavyhearted, feeling the pressures of holiday expectations. Your light touch and loving heart can make things flow more easily. You can bring a ray of hope to a gloomy situation or lighten a tense atmosphere by spreading love and laughter wherever you go.

It can be as simple as smiling as you hold a door open for someone. If a friend is feeling low, surprise her with a care package of small amusements: gold stars for being good, bubble bath, and a chocolate heart. Share the joy of living with loved ones.

Christmas is most truly Christmas when we celebrate it by giving the light of love to those who need it most.

RUTH CARTER STAPLETON

87
Go to a Concert

Music is an essential at Christmastime. And there is so much glorious music to listen to during this time of year. From the magnificence of Handel's *Messiah* to a children's choir at your local church; from a jazz trio playing carols in a restaurant to a showy Christmas spectacular, there are plenty of places to go hear seasonal music.

Music

Go to at least one concert or Christmas program in December. Make it a special occasion and break away from your daily life. Dress up and go out for dinner before a concert. As you sink back into your theater seat, let your cares fly away on musical wings.

Buy holiday season tickets for two in the cheap seats and invite a different friend to each concert to share the joy of music.

Shout praises to the LORD! Sing him a new song of praise when his loyal people meet.

PSALM 149:1 CEV

Eternal Harmony

There is a music wherever there is a harmony, order, or proportion; and thus far we may maintain the music of the spheres; for those well-ordered motions, and regular paces, though they give no sound unto the ear, yet to the understanding they strike a note most full of harmony.

SIR THOMAS BROWNE

88
Take a Winter Walk

Even if the weather outside is frightful, a winter walk can be delightful. Getting outside is good for body and soul. Stretch your legs and leave behind your long list of things that must be done. Bundle up for whatever weather is going on outside, and take yourself out for a winter walk.

Enjoy the outline of bare branches against a winter sky. Revel in a rare sunny day, and look up at the heavenly blue sky to give yourself a larger and brighter perspective on life. Take delight in the crunch of snow under your feet, and catch snowflakes on your tongue during snow showers.

The whine of cold snow underfoot is winter music, like nothing else in the world.

HAL BORLAND

Move

Have hot soup simmering on the back burner or in a slow cooker to warm you up after your chilly walk. Prepare hot chocolate or hot spiced cider.

89

Take Comfort in Familiar Customs

Repeat

❧

Take some quiet
time alone to savor
a favorite private
Christmas ritual, such
as reading the
Christmas story
or decorating a
special corner of
the house.

You and your mom always bake spritz cookies when you arrive at your childhood home for Christmas vacation. Even though you're all grown up, stockings are still hung by the chimney with care. You and your best friend wait till after Christmas to exchange presents and catch up on all the holiday news. Daddy always reads from the Gospel of Luke on Christmas Eve.

Take pleasure in familiar rituals at Christmas. Find comfort in old family customs and let soothing reminders of Christmases past comfort your heart today. Though new experiences are wonderful, there's something deeply nurturing about the old and familiar ways.

The very commonplaces of life are components of its eternal mystery.

GERTRUDE ATHERTON

Illumination

The only lightless dark is the night of
darkness in ignorance and insensibility.

HELEN KELLER

What in me is dark
Illumine, what is low
raise and support . . .

JOHN MILTON

90

Go Look at Christmas Lights

Twinkle

☙

Pick a night to drive around the neighborhood and enjoy the festive look of the houses. When you decide on your favorite, write a note to the homeowners thanking them for helping you celebrate the season.

☙

One of the simple delights of the season is seeing houses all decked out in Christmas lights. Garish flashing light displays and more genteel decorating styles all express the individuality of the homeowners who love to say "Merry Christmas" in lights. Go out and enjoy this neighborhood festival of lights.

Stay late enough after work or shopping to enjoy the lights downtown, too. If you live near waterways, many ships and boats are often decked out in lights. Check out tourist destinations in town that feature light displays. On a clear night look up at the star-spangled display of lights and think of the star over Bethlehem.

One small candle may light a thousand.

William Bradford

91

Visit the Sick and Elderly

You may think you're the one who's giving, but you'll receive even greater gifts from those you visit. The sick and the elderly may be closer to eternity than those who are involved with the daily commerce of life. Take some time out of your busy life to spend time with those who in their adversity may be more attuned to God's presence.

Go to a hospital or nursing home. Sit with someone who is hungry for a human touch and a listening ear. Their courage will inspire you. Take time to pay attention to the stories of your elders and you'll discover timeless wisdom.

Old age is that night of life, as night is the old age of day. Still night is full of magnificence and, for many, it is more brilliant than the day.

ANNE-SOPHIE SWETCHINE

Caring

Gather a few friends who love to sing and go caroling at a local nursing home. Or bring a treasury of Christmas stories and poems to read aloud.

❧

Eternal Love

We miss the purport of Christ's birth if we do not accept it as a living link which joins us together in spirit as children of the ever-living and true God. In love alone—the love of God and the love of man—will be found the solution of all the ills which afflict the world today. Slowly, sometimes painfully, but always with increasing purpose, emerges the great message of Christianity: Only with wisdom comes joy, and with greatness comes love.

HARRY S TRUMAN

92

Bake a Birthday Cake for Jesus

Christmas is a birthday celebration for Jesus. Children love parties, and you can celebrate the birth of Christ with a birthday party, complete with cake and candles. Center a party around the "Happy Birthday, Jesus" theme and delight children—and the young at heart—by blowing out the candles and making a birthday wish for the whole world.

Bake or buy a birthday cake for a December dessert or bring a decorated cake to a potluck. Even a cupcake with a single candle can be a reminder to make a wish, blow out a candle, and thank God for his Son, Jesus Christ.

Away in a manger, no crib for his bed, the little Lord Jesus laid down his sweet head. The stars in the bright sky looked down where he lay, the little Lord Jesus, asleep on the hay.

AUTHOR UNKNOWN

Jesus

Let everybody sing "Happy Birthday" to baby Jesus. Have the youngest child blow out the candles.

93

Use Your Best China

Elegance

Have a candlelight dinner. Arrange candles on the table and around the room. Turn out the lights and enjoy the glowing atmosphere.

Though casual, no-fuss entertaining is fun, Christmas is also a time when you can bring the best china out of the closet where it has been hiding all year. There is a special pleasure in taking extra care to create a beautiful table, honoring the spirit of the season.

Spread the table with your best linen and lace. Create a gorgeous centerpiece of greens, flowers, and shining ornaments. Bring out the crystal goblets, Grandmother's heirloom cut glass, and the most elegant special-occasion china you have. Make place cards and use napkin rings. Light candles and enjoy a meal that's made even more delicious by the beautiful setting.

Bring the same consideration to the preparation of your food as you devote to your appearance. Let your dinner be a poem, like your dress.

CHARLES PIERRE MONSELET

94

Keep Christmas in Your Heart

Christmas is the season of the heart. It all began in love, when the heavenly Father sent Jesus Christ to earth. Mother Mary holding the newborn infant in her arms is a picture of Christmas held close to the heart.

Honor

Keep Christmas in your heart by honoring the spirit. Resolve to be a more loving and compassionate person in the coming year. Thank God for the gift of life. Remember that this birth two thousand years ago affected the world in ways that could never be imagined on that first Christmas night. It is in love that Christmas begins, and it goes on forever.

Set aside some time to meditate on the birth of Christ. Think about simple ways you are free to love others because God first loved you.

The only real blind person at Christmastime is he who has not Christmas in his heart.

HELEN KELLER

Timeless Gifts

As the Magi came bearing gifts, so do we also; gifts that relieve want, gifts that are sweet and fragrant with friendship, gifts that breathe love, gifts that mean service, gifts inspired by the star that shone over the City of David nearly two thousand years ago.

KATE DOUGLAS WIGGIN

95

Sing Carols and Hymns

The Christmas songs are so familiar. You hear recordings and professional performances all through the season. Add your voice to the chorus of voices singing carols and hymns. Even if you "can't carry a tune," at Christmas hearts in tune with one another make the melody true and sweet.

Buy a Christmas songbook. Sing all the verses of your favorite carols with gusto as you clean the house. Sing along with the radio as you drive. Join in at church when hymns are sung. Make a melody with your voice, and you'll discover there's a song in your heart.

The shepherds sing,
and shall I silent be?

GEORGE HERBERT

Harmonize

Read stories about how favorite Christmas carols came to be. "Silent Night" is even more meaningful when you know why Josef Mohr and Franz Gruber wrote the words and music.

96
Leave Room in Your Schedule

Remember that a visit with your mother or a special dinner with your children is just as important as the office party. Leave room for those you love the most.

Take control of your calendar instead of allowing a busy holiday schedule to control you. When you're tempted to pack your days with too many activities and too many people, deliberately block out some empty space on your calendar. This will leave room for necessary downtime—or for unexpected opportunities or emergencies.

Make an appointment with yourself to spend a couple of hours doing whatever for an afternoon. If you have a tight schedule one day, balance it the next day with a more flexible and open schedule. Planning ahead to give yourself bonus time makes life easier and more enjoyable during the holidays.

Come to me, all you who are weary and burdened, and I will give you rest.

MATTHEW 11:28 NIV

In His Presence

Indeed, if Christ became Man, it is because He wanted to be any man and every man. If we believe in the Incarnation of the Son of God, there should be no one on earth in whom we are not prepared to see, in mystery, the presence of Christ.

THOMAS MERTON

97

Live in the Presence of God

Focus

Make a decision to surrender to God, and commit to living your life wholeheartedly in his presence.

Here is a simple way to listen to your heart and be aware of God's presence in your daily life. Take a second to breathe deeply. Now focus your thoughts and become aware that God loves you and is with you at all times, as close and intimate as your beating heart.

This can be done in the midst of a busy day to help you stay connected to your spirit as you do simple tasks, such as wrapping gifts or washing dishes. Practicing the presence of God reminds you that everything you do has meaning and purpose when done with prayer and awareness.

Rejoice always, pray without ceasing, in everything give thanks; for this is the will of God in Christ Jesus for you.

1 Thessalonians 5:16–18 nkjv

98
Make a Christmas Treasure Box

Every Christmas brings its memories—and its treasures. Each year you bring out cherished ornaments, beloved heirlooms. Each year a new memory is created then packed away till the next Christmas comes around. Make a Christmas treasure box in which to store those happy mementos.

Collect

Christmas treasures may include the star for the top of the tree from your first Christmas together, a child or grandchild's gilded macaroni angel, or a handblown glass ornament you found on vacation. The treasure box may be just plain cardboard or beautifully decorated, but it will keep the blessings and memories of Christmas safe from year to year.

Label each treasure you pack away so you can remember who gave it to you, why it's special, and which Christmas it came into your life.

Along with Christmas belong the keepsakes and the customs. Those humble, everyday things a mother clings to, and ponders, like Mary in the secret spaces of her heart.

MARJORIE HOLMES

Benediction

May the light of Christ's love surround you. May the majesty of the stars in a clear night sky remind you that God is guiding you as he did the wise men who sought the child. May you always remember that the presence and mercy of God are with you at all times. May grace and gratitude over-flow. And may the joy of Christmas live in your heart all year round.

AMEN

99

Celebrate Epiphany

Epiphany comes from the Greek word for "unveiling" and "revelation." The Feast of Epiphany on January 6 is also known as the Feast of Lights, celebrating the revelation of Christ as the Light of the World. It's the culmination of the twelve days of Christmas, and it is a celebration that is more ancient than the Christmas Day feast.

Celebrate Epiphany by having a house blessing to begin the new year. Many people wait till that day to take decorations down. Light candles and have a small feast to commemorate the visit of the wise men who came to worship the baby born in Bethlehem.

> *Jerusalem, stand up! Shine! Your new day is dawning. The glory of the LORD shines brightly on you.*
>
> ISAIAH 60:1 CEV

Resolve

Write down five things you've always wanted to do or learn. Choose one as a New Year's resolution, then take the steps to make it happen.

100

Praise the Lord

Praise

Send a thank-you note praising someone who has influenced your life in positive ways, such as a favorite teacher or a beloved relative.

Christmas brings the gift of God's love. When so many good gifts are given, it's as natural as breathing to want to thank the giver. Thank God for the good things you have received. Thank him not only for daily blessings, but also for his presence in your life. Praise him because he is worthy of praise.

And when there are difficult times, losses, and questions that cannot be answered by any human being, again go to the Lord, knowing that you will find compassion and encouragement in God's loving presence.

Let everything that has breath praise the LORD. Praise the LORD!

PSALM 150:6 NKJV

101

Celebrate Christmas Year-Round

The spirit of Christmas is love. Gift giving, gathering together with friends and loved ones, singing, having fun, giving time and talents to the greater community—all can be shared throughout the year. You don't have to wait for a certain time of year to share love and caring with others.

Recognize that each day is a gift and see each person as a reflection of the Christ who comes to earth to bring peace and reconciliation. Thank God for the opportunity to love and serve the people he came to love and serve, and you'll cradle Christmas in your heart all year round.

For Christ is born and born again,
When His love lives in hearts of men.

W. D. DORRITY

Spirit

Share love by teaching your skill: a carpenter teaches woodworking; a musician offers guitar lessons; a cook demonstrates making gourmet dishes.

145